T32479

Thomas A. EDISON

Paul Mason

RAINTREE
STECK-VAUGHN
RSVP® PUBLISHERS

A Harcourt Company

Austin   New York
www.raintreesteckvaughn.com

Published by Raintree Steck-Vaughn Publishers, an imprint of Steck-Vaughn Company

Library of Congress Cataloging-in-Publication Data is available upon request.

 ISBN 0-7398-4414-8

Picture Acknowledgments: Archive Photos 13, 30, 41; Robert Harding Picture Collection 15, 17, 22 (bottom), 32, 36, 38, 40, 43; Hodder Wayland Picture Library 4, 19, 23, 24, 25, 26, 27, 28, 31; Hulton Getty Picture Library 34; Peter Newark 5, 6, 7 (bottom), 10, 12, 20, 22 (top); Mary Evans Picture Library 7 (top), 14, 18, 29, 35, 37; Photri 8 (top and bottom), 11, 16, 33, 42, 44; Popperfoto 39.

Printed in Italy. Bound in the United States.

1 2 3 4 5 6 7 8 9 0 LB 05 04 03 02 01

Contents

Electric Power!

IT WAS 2:45 P.M. on September 4, 1882, and a group of
New York City's most powerful and influential men were
gathered in the offices of J. Pierpoint Morgan, the famous
banker and one of the richest men in the world. Tension filled
the air. Each of the men stole glances first at their watches,
then at one another, and finally at the glass bulbs that were
arranged on one side of the room. Some of the men had sunk
hundreds of thousands of dollars into Mr. Edison's latest
project, which was the first commercial, electric power supply.
They were about to find out if it worked.

BELOW: *The dynamo room of
Edison's first electric lighting
station, in 1882.*

Meanwhile, just a block or two away at 255 Pearl Street, feverish activity was taking place. This building was home to Edison's electric lighting station and at 3 P.M., it was due to light up offices and buildings around the area for the first time. As the moment approached, the engineers realized that there was no more they could do. In the power station and in Mr. Morgan's office, all eyes were on the clock as it dragged slowly toward 3 P.M. Then the moment came.

The bulbs in Mr. Morgan's office flickered. Dimly at first, they began to glow with a strong, steady light. Across the 1.2 square miles (2 sq km) surrounding Edison's lighting station, similar bulbs glowed in the offices and factories of his thirty or so other customers. They were the first of many people to experience the wonder of an electric power supply.

Who Was Edison?

Thomas A. Edison was one of the greatest inventors the world has ever known. When Edison was born, the world had no radios, no typewriters, no telephones, no way of recording music, no movies…very few of the inventions we take for granted today. By the time Edison died in 1931, all these things existed, and most of them had grown out of his inventions.

IN THEIR OWN WORDS

"The point at which I am different from most other inventors is that I have, besides the usual inventor's makeup, a bump of practicality…the sense of the business, money value of an invention."

EDISON, DESCRIBING HIS BUSINESS SENSE.

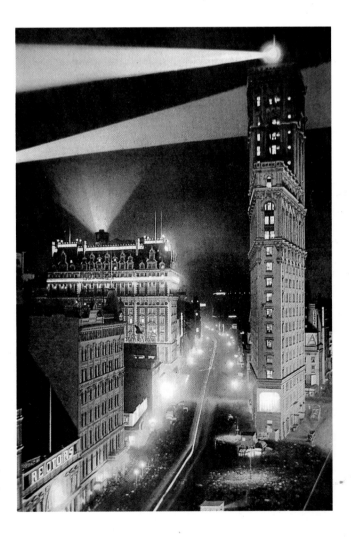

RIGHT: *An early photograph of the Flatiron building in New York City in 1910, just 28 years after Edison first brought electric power to the city.*

The Nineteenth–Century United States

EDISON WAS BORN in Ohio in 1847. The world at this time was a dynamic, exciting place and during the last half the end of the 19th century, there were few countries more exciting than the United States.

In the north, large factories were springing up as the country's natural resources were used to support manufacturing businesses. Great railways linked both coasts of the United States, allowing people and goods to be transported back and forth, and the telegraph allowed people to communicate quickly over long distances. More and more people moved to the cities, where they were able to get jobs.

Pushing all this growth forward was a great movement of scientific and technological progress.

BELOW: *Steam trains such as this one allowed people to move across the U.S. to the west during the 19th century.*

The Civil War

In 1861, civil war broke out between the northern and southern states. In many ways, the war mirrored other changes in American life. The increasingly powerful, industrial northern states fought against the largely rural southern states. The North's victory in 1865 reflected the way in which the United States was becoming a world industrial power during the 19th century.

ABOVE: *An iron and steel works in Pennsylvania, typical of northern industry in the U.S. in the mid-19th century.*

BELOW: *One of the many battles of the American Civil War, the Battle of Spotsylvania Court House, May 1864.*

The Age of Invention

The 19th century gave birth to many of the inventions we associate with modern life, including the telephone, the automobile, electric power, and moving pictures. Usually, they resulted from breakthroughs by scientists and engineers. New inventions came thick and fast, though some were not as useful as others. Many useless inventions were advertised alongside ones that would turn out to be truly useful.

Early Years

Edison's Childhood

Thomas Alva Edison arrived in the world on February 11,
1847, in Milan, a small town near the shore of Lake Erie, in
the state of Ohio. His parents were Canadians living in the
U.S. They had already had six children, but three died before
Thomas was born. He was so weak when he was born that
his mother was sure he would die, too.

When Thomas was seven, his family moved to Port
Huron, a larger town on the southern tip of Lake Huron, in
the state of Michigan. At school in Port Huron, Thomas had
a very hard time. He had trouble with his hearing, and his
teacher thought he was slow. Like many teachers of the
time, he thought he could beat knowledge into his students.
Thomas stayed at the bottom of the class for three months,

ABOVE: *A portrait of Edison as
a young boy of about eight.*

BELOW: *A modern-day photo of
the house in which Edison was
born, in Milan, Ohio.*

until his mother took him out of school. She had been a schoolteacher herself before marrying Thomas's father, so she decided to teach him at home.

School of Natural Philosophy

Thomas was an avid reader, who read Shakespeare, history books, and the Bible. His favorite book was *School of Natural Philosophy*, which suggested simple scientific experiments to do at home. Thomas did them all. He built his own laboratory in his bedroom, but was forced to move it to the basement because of the mess caused by some of his experiments (particularly the explosions!).

IN THEIR OWN WORDS

"My mother taught me how to read good books quickly and correctly, and as this opened up a great world in literature, I have always been very thankful for this early training."

EDISON IN HIS LATER YEARS, REMEMBERING HIS EARLY EDUCATION.

"That boy is addled [stupid]."

EDISON'S SCHOOLTEACHER, IN 1855.

THE RAILWAY EXPERIMENTER

In 1859, a new railway line opened that linked Port Huron to Detroit. At the age of 12, Thomas got a job selling newspapers on the trains. He soon sold fruits and candy as well, to make a bit of extra money.

Thomas set up a laboratory in a corner of an empty luggage car and used his spare time to continue his experiments. Unfortunately, one day an experiment got out of hand and the laboratory caught fire. Edison later remembered that the guard, who was burned putting out the fire, pulled him by the ears as a result!

Read All About It!

In 1861, while Thomas was still working on the trains, the American Civil War broke out. On April 6, 1862, word reached Detroit of a terrible battle being fought at a place

BELOW: *The Battle of Shiloh began on April 6, 1862. By April 7 there would be over 20,000 men lying dead or wounded on the battlefield.*

IN THEIR OWN WORDS

"[A guard] took me by the ears and lifted me. I felt something snap inside my head. My deafness started from that time and has ever since progressed."

EDISON IN LATER YEARS, DATING THE BEGINNING OF HIS
DEAFNESS FROM HIS DAYS AS A NEWSPAPER BOY.

called Shiloh. Thomas sensed that if word of the battle reached people at stations on the way to Port Huron, everyone would want to read about it and he'd sell more newspapers. So he persuaded the Detroit telegraph operator to send a short telegram to each station. Then he raced to the newspaper offices.

Thomas normally only bought a hundred papers, but this time he wanted 1,000 copies. However, he only had enough money to buy 300 so he had to persuade the editor to let him have them on credit. This was quite a gamble for Thomas to take, because he had no real way of paying back the credit if he didn't sell the papers.

Luckily for Thomas, he was right. At the first station, where he normally sold two papers, Thomas sold 200. At the next, he sold 300 and decided to put up the price. By the time the train reached home in Port Huron, all the papers were sold and Thomas had made a big profit.

BELOW: *Thomas as a newsboy on the railroad.*

IN THEIR OWN WORDS

"The happiest time in my life was when I was 12 years old. I was just old enough to have a good time in the world, but not old enough to understand any of its troubles."

EDISON IN 1930, REMEMBERING HIS CHILDHOOD.

THE TELEGRAPH

While working on the Port Huron-to-Detroit line, Edison got to know the telegraph operator, James MacKenzie. Thomas was already interested in telegraphs. He had built a simple version to connect his best friend's house with his own. MacKenzie taught him how to use the type of telegraph found in telegraph offices all around the world.

BELOW: *A telegraph line being constructed beside a railway track in the 1860s. By the end of the nineteenth century, telegraph lines had been put up across large areas of empty country in the U.S., connecting communities and sending news of national events.*

Edison the Telegrapher

In the early 1860s, telegraph operators were in great demand, partly because many experienced operators had gone to work for the armies in the American Civil War. As a "tramp" telegrapher, it was possible to travel around the country, working somewhere for a few months, and then moving on somewhere else. To an adventurous young man like Edison, the chance was too good to miss. In 1863, at the age of 16, he decided to become a tramp telegrapher.

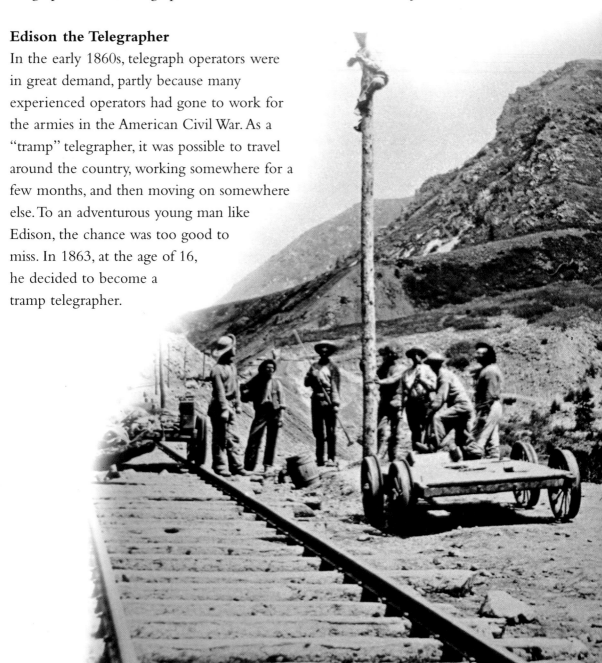

Edison never stopped experimenting. As a telegraph operator, he liked the night shift best, which left the day free for his experiments. The night shift helped develop one of his first inventions. Night operators were supposed to send a signal every half-hour to show that they were awake. Edison, tired from a hard day's inventing, needed to sleep, so he created a device that sent the signal automatically. It worked perfectly, until his bosses found out and he was fired.

IN THEIR OWN WORDS

"I built a telegraph wire between our houses… The wire was [the one] that [was] used for suspending stove pipes, the insulators were small bottles pegged on ten-penny nails driven into trees. It worked fine."

EDISON REMEMBERING THE TELEGRAPH SYSTEM HE MADE BETWEEN HIS FRIEND'S HOME AND HIS OWN.

THE TELEGRAPH

Telegraphs used electric currents sent along a wire to send messages from place to place. Telegraph operators tapped a lever with their hand to start the current. At the other end, the current was heard as a click. Pressing the lever down for a longer time made a long click, whereas a short press made a short click. The sender sent a message using the Morse code, where the clicks stood for letters of the alphabet.

AN EARLY TELEGRAPH TRANSMITTER AND RECEIVER

Receiver

Electric coil

Sending key

THE MOVE TO BOSTON

In 1868, after four years as a tramp telegrapher, 21-year-old Edison arrived in Boston and got a job with the Western Union Telegraph Company. On his first day, the other telegraph operators looked at the scruffy young man and thought he must be a young, inexperienced operator who needed to learn how quickly things were done in the big city. They set him up to receive messages from a press operator in New York. Press operators were the fastest in the business and Edison knew it, but he didn't say a word. He was a first-class operator himself.

The messages started to come over the wire at an alarming speed, but Edison kept up. Finally, in desperation, the operator at the other end started using abbreviations. Edison interrupted him and sent back the sarcastic message: "You seem to be tired. Suppose you send a little while with

BELOW: *State Street in Boston, about 1840. By the time Edison arrived in 1868, Boston had grown into a bigger, much busier city.*

FIRST INVENTIONS

One of Edison's first inventions was an electronic vote counter for the U.S. Congress. The counter worked perfectly, but there was one problem—Congress didn't want to buy it. Edison learned a hard lesson: it's no good inventing things that no one wants, because they don't make any money.

Another invention was much more successful: Edison's "stock ticker." This was a telegraph-based device that transmitted news of changes in the values of stocks and shares. The news was printed out on long strips of paper, called "ticker tape." This information was valuable to banks and other financial groups, who were willing to pay for it.

EDISON'S FIRST STOCK TICKER

Ticker tape shows prices

your other foot?" The room exploded with laughter. Edison had suggested the operator was using his foot to tap out the messages instead of his hand.

Trouble

In the middle of the 19th century, Boston was the center of the U.S.'s scientific community. When he wasn't working at the Western Union, Edison was working on his experiments in the workshop of Charles Williams's Electrical Shop on Court Street. But Edison didn't stay in Boston long. Later in 1868, he got into trouble with his superiors at Western Union by writing down the messages in tiny letters which were hard to read. When told to write bigger, Edison responded by writing all his messages in very large letters. Immediately demoted, Edison walked out.

TO NEW YORK

In 1869, Edison moved to New York City. He arrived with nothing, not even a place to stay, but he was quickly back in the inventing business. Soon after he arrived, Edison met with Franklin Pope, who worked for the Gold Indicator Company. This company had invented the gold indicator, the very first stock ticker, which showed the changing prices for buying and selling gold. One day at Pope's office, the gold indicator broke down. There was a panic—no one knew what to do—until Edison calmly fixed the machine within two hours.

BELOW: *New York City's Broadway, in 1887. By this time it was (and still is) one of the best known streets in the United States.*

The New York office of the Western Union Telegraph Company asked Edison to sort out a problem with its transmitting equipment. Edison found a solution fairly quickly and Western Union asked to buy the device he had invented. Edison visited their offices. He wanted $5,000, but hardly dared to ask for so much money. While Edison hesitated, the Western Union representative offered $40,000 for the device. "This caused me to come as near to fainting as I ever got," Edison later said.

IN THEIR OWN WORDS

"People here come and buy without your soliciting [trying to sell]."

EDISON, WRITING ABOUT NEW YORK TO A FRIEND BACK IN BOSTON.

A New Laboratory

Edison used his windfall to start a laboratory and factory in Newark, New Jersey, producing stock tickers and other equipment. In 1871, on Christmas Day, he married Mary Stillwell, whom he had met earlier that year, when she came to work at the factory. Some stories say that after the wedding, Edison went back to his laboratory and stayed there until midnight, to finish an experiment he had started.

The "Invention Factory"

In 1876 Edison moved again, to the small settlement of Menlo Park, New Jersey. By this time, he and Mary had a four-year-old daughter, Marion. In Menlo Park, Edison gathered together skilled craftspeople who would be able to make parts for his inventions. Their aim was to bring out an invention every ten days and what Edison called a "big trick" every six months.

King of the Patents

Edison wasn't just a great inventor. He was also good at making sure he got the credit (and the profit) for his inventions. In his lifetime, Edison took out 1,093 patents on new ideas.

RIGHT: *Mary Stillwell married Edison in 1871.*

The Great Inventions

"I am so deaf that I am debarred from hearing all the finer articulations [words], and have to depend on the judgement of others."

EDISON TELLING A JOURNALIST ABOUT HIS HEARING DIFFICULTIES IN 1877.

BELOW: *Alexander Graham Bell is the first to use the New York–Chicago telephone link in 1892.*

The Telephone

In 1876, news reached the world that a Scotsman named Alexander Graham Bell had succeeded in transmitting the human voice through a wire. The first telephone had been created. Western Union immediately asked Edison to see if he could improve on the device, which wasn't able to work over long distances.

On the face of it, Western Union might have seemed crazy to ask Edison to improve on the telephone. Edison, after all, was practically deaf by now and could barely hear normal conversations. He was only able to go to the theater (one of his favorite pastimes) if he could get front-row seats, and his assistants quite often had to bellow at him to be heard. Was this really the right man to improve a device that required its users to listen to words transmitted through down a wire?

Nonetheless, the Western Union president, William Orton, thought Edison was the right man for the job. He called Edison "probably the best electro-mechanician in the country." There was also the fact that by asking Edison to improve the telephone, Western Union was enlisting the help not just of Edison, but also his team of assistants. Menlo Park was the largest private laboratory in the United States, and Edison had hired some very clever people to work there. All of them would help solve the problem of the telephone.

The very first telephones had several problems. They used the same device for sending and receiving, so you could not listen if you were talking. Also, the signal they sent on the wire was weak and would not carry far. It was these areas that Edison hoped to improve.

LEFT: *Edison (middle-row, center) and his chief assistants from the Menlo Park laboratory.*

HOW BELL'S TELEPHONE WORKED

The human voice produces vibrations in the air, which produce similar vibrations in a thin sheet, or diaphragm, of iron. In Bell's telephone, a diaphragm is placed near a magnet. The magnet has a coil of wire wound around it. In the sending instrument, or transmitter, the diaphragm vibrates in response to the voice and an electric signal is produced in the coil of wire. The signal travels to the receiving telephone and varies the magnetism, so that the diaphragm there vibrates in the same way, reproducing the original sound.

Mouthpiece

Coil of wire

Rubber case

Ends of wires connected to coil

Bar magnet

Diaphragm of soft iron

EDISON'S TELEPHONE

Edison used to say that being deaf was an excellent way of making sure his new telephone finally worked. If he could hear it, it must be loud and clear! The Menlo Park team worked long hours trying to improve the telephone. Often Edison didn't go home until breakfast time, and his employees were expected to work just as hard. He once locked the doors and told them that they couldn't leave until the job was finished! Edison's wife, Mary, found this to be a difficult time. There were few people in Menlo Park apart from the workers and she felt so scared without her husband in the house that she slept with a pistol under her pillow.

By 1877, at the age of 30, Edison was ready to demonstrate his new, improved telephone. He and his assistants had made two primary improvements to Bell's original design. First the transmitter was separated from the receiver, so it was possible to interrupt someone at the other end of the line, if one caller didn't agree with what the other was saying! Secondly, the new telephone could be used over greater distances. Many of the telephones we use today work on exactly the same principles as Edison's improved version.

LEFT: *An illustration of the Menlo Park laboratories.*

Despite his success with the telephone, Edison, though famous in the scientific community, was still not a household name. The invention that would make him truly famous was just around the corner, and the story starts (on the next page) with a child's toy.

HOW EDISON'S TELEPHONE WORKED

Edison's telephone had the same receiver as Bell's, but a different sending instrument, or transmitter. In Bell's telephone, all the power came from the voice of a person speaking. In Edison's telephone, the power came from a battery, which produced an electric current.

The new transmitter was much more effective in turning voice vibrations into electric pulses. A diaphragm inside the transmitter formed the side of a box containing carbon granules. When the diaphragm vibrated, the electrical resistance between the granules varied, changing the current produced by the battery.

Carbon granules

Diaphragm

ABOVE: *An advertisement for the Edison Talking Doll.*

BELOW: *From right to left, Edison, Charles Batchelor, and Uriah Painter in 1878, when they went to Washington to demonstrate the phonograph.*

THE PHONOGRAPH

While working on the design for the telephone, Edison made a toy for his daughter, Marion. It used a carbon diaphragm, like the ones used in telephones, to respond to the vibrations of a human voice. The movement of the diaphragm provided electrical power for a model of a man sawing wood. Edison began to think that perhaps if the movement of the diaphragm could be recorded in some way, it might be possible to make the diaphragm reproduce the original sound using the same movement.

Soon, Edison had a working model of his "phonograph," or "sound writer." The device was named after the Ancient Greek words *phonos*, meaning "sound," and *graph*, meaning "writing." Edison demonstrated it to his assistants by playing them a recording of himself reciting the child's nursery rhyme "Mary Had A Little Lamb." His assistants were amazed, and the rest of the United States—indeed, the rest of the world—was soon to follow.

"The Wizard of Menlo Park"

The phonograph quickly caught the public's attention. Exhibitions and demonstrations were organized, at which people paid 25¢ to hear the phonograph in action. A novelty model was sold for $30, which was a huge amount in those days. This was quickly withdrawn because Edison planned to charge even more for his "standard" version and didn't want people to buy the cheaper one. The world was gripped by Edison-mania: In Europe and America, people were desperate to find out more about the man the press called "The Wizard of Menlo Park." Edison even went to Washington, D.C., to demonstrate his phonograph to President Rutherford Hayes.

HOW THE PHONOGRAPH WORKED

The phonograph had a diaphragm behind a mouthpiece. Sound made the diaphragm vibrate, which moved a needle attached to its center. The needle made dents on a drum covered with tin foil. When the needle was passed back over the dents, the diaphragm recreated the original sound. It was such a simple idea that Alexander Graham Bell, the inventor of the telephone, said it was "a most astonishing thing to me that I could possibly have let this invention slip through my fingers."

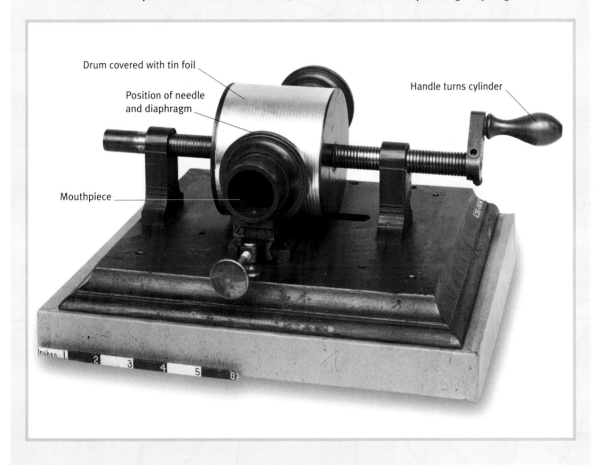

Drum covered with tin foil

Position of needle and diaphragm

Handle turns cylinder

Mouthpiece

Inches 1 2 3 4 5 6

Tired out, in 1878 Edison took his first holiday since his honeymoon in 1871. He traveled to Wyoming to see the total eclipse of the sun in July, then on to San Francisco, Yosemite, and then Nevada. But, in the back of his mind, Edison was probably already thinking about his next big project: the light bulb.

ELECTRIC LIGHT

In the 19th century, the gas companies were among the most powerful in the United States. Apart from oil and candles, they were the main source of lighting to homes and businesses in America's cities. Edison saw that if he could challenge the gas companies, he might become a very wealthy man.

He formed the Edison Electric Company with the aim of supplying electric light instead. The announcement that Edison planned to compete with the gas companies sparked

IN THEIR OWN WORDS

"Genius is one percent inspiration and 99 percent perspiration."

ONE OF EDISON'S MOST FAMOUS QUOTES, DESCRIBING THE PROCESS OF INVENTING.

RIGHT: *An artist's impression of assistants at Menlo Park, trying to carbonize a filament for an electric light bulb.*

T 32479

a stockmarket crash. In late 1878, the value of shares in the gas companies suddenly dropped by 25 to 30 percent, as investors raced to get rid of them before Edison put the gas companies out of business.

To produce electric light, the main problem facing Edison was to find a suitable material for the filament. After trying thousands of substances, an African–American scientist, Lewis Latimer, working for Edison, made a good filament by carbonizing small pieces of paper. Edison also had to set up a glass-blowing factory to produce light bulbs, and make a machine that created a vacuum inside them.

Finally, Edison was able to make a light bulb that lasted long enough to be useful. By Christmas 1878, crowds from across the U.S. were flocking to Menlo Park. Edison's laboratory and home were lit up like beacons using electric light bulbs, or "incandescent lamps" as they were also called.

HOW THE LIGHT BULB WORKED

Early light bulbs were very like those we use today. They were made up of a sealed glass bulb with a vacuum inside. Inside the bulb was a thin filament, which would heat up and glow when electricity passed through it, providing light.

Glass bulb

Carbon filament

Vacuum

ELECTRIC POWER

"We're striking it big in the electric light, better than my vivid imagination first conceived. Where this thing is going to stop, Lord only knows."

EDISON IN OCTOBER 1879, BEFORE HIS NEW COMPANY EVEN HAD AN OFFICE OF ITS OWN.

Having created the light bulb, Edison now had to find a way of producing electric power. By the summer of 1879, Edison and his team had invented a generator that turned steam into electricity far more efficiently than any other. Because of its strange shape they called it "Long-legged Mary-Anne."

Work continued on other uses of electric power. In May 1880, Edison demonstrated an electric train in the grounds of Menlo Park. Guests had to hang on tight as the train whizzed over bumps and through turns at 25 miles (40 km) per hour, but the return journey wasn't half as exciting. The train broke down and the guests had to push it home.

Edison Electric Light Company

In 1880 Edison bought two buildings on Pearl Street in Lower Manhattan, New York, to be the base for the Edison Electric Light Company. By the spring of 1881, he and his family had moved from Menlo Park to a rented house on Gramercy Lane, so that Edison could be nearer his newest business. He was convinced it was going to be a great success.

In 1882, the Edison Electric Light Company began to supply power to nearby businesses. This early power could only be supplied within a 2.5 mile (40 km) radius. Even so, within a short time electric power stations had sprung up across the United States. (See pages 4–5 for details about the day the lights were first switched on.)

LEFT: *Edison's super-efficient generator, the "Long-legged Mary-Anne," was at the heart of his success. It converted more energy into electricity than other dynamos at the time.*

PARALLEL CIRCUITS

Edison's wiring for his new electricity-supply business used parallel circuits, where each lamp only receives a fraction of the total current. This meant that it was possible for one part of the circuit to be turned off without stopping the electricity supply to all the other parts.

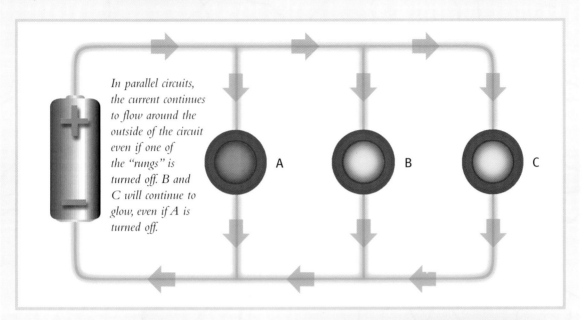

In parallel circuits, the current continues to flow around the outside of the circuit even if one of the "rungs" is turned off. B and C will continue to glow, even if A is turned off.

A   B   C

IN THEIR OWN WORDS

"I have accomplished all that I promised."

EDISON TO REPORTERS AFTER HIS PEARL STREET POWER STATION BEGAN WORK ON SEPTEMBER 4, 1882.

RIGHT: *Edison driving the electric train that ran on the grounds of his Menlo Park laboratory.*

Inventor and Businessman

Mary Edison Dies

By 1884, Edison was a famous inventor and a wealthy man with a thriving business. Then tragedy struck. His wife Mary caught typhoid and died. Edison was racked with grief. He couldn't bear to go back to his house in Menlo Park, so the family moved permanently into an apartment on East 18th Street in Manhattan.

Mina Miller

The next summer, Edison met 20-year-old Mina Miller. He was captivated. Mina was beautiful and lively, as well as being a college graduate (which was unusual for a woman at that time). Edison taught Mina the Morse code so that they could speak to each other privately even when there were other people around. During a carriage ride one day, he tapped out the question "Will you marry me?" on her hand. A breathless wait followed, until she tapped back a message on his hand: "Yes." For the rest of their lives, the two communicated in Morse when they wanted to hold private conversations.

RIGHT: *Mina Miller, who was Edison's second wife.*

IN THEIR OWN WORDS

"[He was] shaking with grief, weeping and sobbing so he could hardly tell me my mother had died in the night."

EDISON'S DAUGHTER MARION, REMEMBERING HER FATHER THE MORNING AFTER HER MOTHER HAD DIED.

Mina often tapped out other people's words on her husband's hand so that he could "hear" what was being said.

West Orange

In 1886, soon after the Edisons returned from their honeymoon, there was a dispute between the managers and workers at the Edison Machine Works, Edison's factory in New York City. As a result, the whole business was moved to Schenectady, in New York state. Only some of the workers kept their jobs.

The Edisons also decided to move out of Manhattan to a house they bought in West Orange, New Jersey. Edison began work on a new laboratory, which was to be ten times the size of the old Menlo Park "invention factory." Once the new laboratory opened, Edison began to oversee a large number of projects at the same time. He had gone from being a full-time inventor to being the head of a large research and development company.

Legal Battles

In 1883, Edison began the first of many legal battles with people whom he felt had copied his inventions. Over the course of his career he would spend over $2 million on such courtroom disputes.

RIGHT: *Edison in his new laboratory.*

"I am experimenting upon an instrument which does for the eye what the phonograph does for the ear, which is the recording and reproduction of things in motion."

EDISON IN 1888.

BELOW: *Edison looking at film that was first developed in the 1880s.*

MOVING PICTURES

In 1888, Edison was visited by a British photographer named Eadweard Muybridge, who wanted to put a sequence of pictures to the accompaniment of phonograph sound. The project didn't work, but it gave Edison the idea of combining his phonograph technology with film. Edison and his assistant, William Dickson, coated a phonograph-type cylinder in light-sensitive film, then put it inside a camera case. Each time a picture was taken of a moving object, the cylinder was turned slightly. Then another picture was taken. Once the film was processed and the sequence of pictures run through a viewer, the audience could see motion.

At about this time, George Eastman invented a new celluloid film that was far less bulky than anything that had been seen before. In 1889, Edison ordered some Eastman film to be cut up into long strips. William Dickson worked out a way of running the film through a camera by turning a crank. Between them the two men had invented the "kinetograph," along with a viewer, the "kinetoscope."

Edison began making movies in the "Black Maria," a black-painted building in West Orange. The building was built on tracks so that it could follow the sunlight, to make filming easier. His first movie with a plot was *The Great Train Robbery*. In the end, over 2,000 films were made in the Black Maria. Among them were the first talking motion pictures and the first color movie (made by hand-painting each frame of the film).

Audiences reacted with panic to the first movies. Not knowing what they were seeing, people watching a film in which a wave broke towards the camera fled from the cinema. They thought the wave was actually coming out of the wall to drown them.

IN THEIR OWN WORDS

"My plan was to synchronize the camera and the phonograph so as to record sounds when the pictures were made, and reproduce the two in harmony… We had the first of the so-called "talking pictures" in our laboratory thirty years ago."

EDISON SPEAKING IN 1925.

T32479

The Twentieth Century

Mining

For a time, as the 19th century drew to a close, it seemed that Edison's touch had deserted him. He became involved in a project to extract iron ore from low-grade deposits in the New Jersey mountains. Iron ore was the basis of much produced in the United States manufacturing industry. If it could be made to work, the new technology would allow iron ore to be mined close to home, instead of having to be brought in from elsewhere.

BELOW: *Edison (standing on the left) on a camping trip in 1918 with some of the most influential men in the United States. From the left, they are Edison, Harvey Firestone Jr., John Burroughs, Henry Ford, Harvey Firestone, and (seated below) R.J.H. de Loach.*

IN THEIR OWN WORDS

"Well, it's all gone, but we had a hell of a good time spending it."

EDISON, AFTER THE FAILURE OF THE IRON-ORE PROJECT.

LEFT: *Edison always found it easy to relax away from "society," either at the mines or on camping trips.*

Edison loved the mining culture. He spent weeks up in the hills with his sleeves rolled up and a dirty face, camping with the miners and working on his ideas. But just as the technology was starting to work, high-grade iron-ore deposits were discovered near Lake Superior, in the Upper Midwest. It was no longer worth mining the low-grade deposits in the East and the mining company went bust. With it went $2 million of Edison's money.

Concrete

Edison's next big project used some of the technology from his mining experiences. He set up a cement works, which used a giant kiln to bake cement blocks. Edison thought that they could be used to build roads or even houses, but the business never became as successful as he hoped.

CARS AND THE ELECTRIC STORAGE BATTERY

IN THEIR OWN WORDS

"I do not know how long it would take to wear out one of the batteries, for we have not been able to exhaust the possibilities of one of them. But I feel sure one will last longer than four or five automobiles."

EDISON TALKING TO THE PRESS ABOUT HIS NEW
ELECTRIC STORAGE BATTERY IN 1903.

ABOVE: *Edison's electric battery was popular for use in vans such as this one because it was so long-lived.*

After the failure of the mining project, Edison thought he might succeed with the car industry. He set himself a simple target: to make an electric battery that would power a car for 100 miles (160 km) at 25 miles (40 km) per hour. It took years, but in 1903 Edison unveiled an electric storage battery, which he claimed was far superior to any other. It also was more expensive.

The manufacture and sale of the Edison battery only began in 1910. Several firms brought out electric cars and trucks that used the battery, and because it lasted for so long, it was especially popular for trucks traveling long distances. However, other firms had also developed electric batteries and Edison's struggled to gain popularity. But the real problem was created by Edison's friend, Henry Ford. In 1908, Ford had brought out his gasoline-driven Model T car. It was by far the cheapest car that had been made, and was hugely popular. Most importantly, it established in the American public mind the idea that cars were driven by gasoline, not electricity.

Edison set his mind to finding other uses for his battery. Soon it was being sold for use in railroad signals, ships and submarines, radios, miners' lamps, and as a back-up power source for businesses and isolated homes. The Edison Storage Battery Company was earning $25,000 a month by 1912, and continued to do well for many more years.

IN THEIR OWN WORDS

"The horse is doomed. The horseless vehicle is the coming wonder."

EDISON IN 1895.

BELOW: *Henry Ford and his son in a Model T car. The Model T was so popular that electric cars did not sell in large enough quantities to be profitable.*

THE WINTER HOME

By 1900, Edison no longer worked nonstop all year round. He often came home for meals on time and, starting in 1901, he and Mina spent every winter in a house he had built in Fort Myers, Florida. Of course Edison had a laboratory there too, so that he could carry on with his experiments. There was also a botanical garden filled with over 300 plants from around the world, many of which were used in Edison's experiments.

BELOW: *Edison with George Eastman, who developed strip film for Edison's kinetoscope in 1888.*

The house in Florida was originally one of two. The other house belonged to Edison's childhood friend Ezra Gilliand. But Gilliand only stayed for a year after the homes were built in 1884. After he helped another inventor defeat Edison in a patent dispute, Edison bought him out and converted the two homes into one.

The house was called Seminole Lodge and, like everything Edison was involved with, it was carefully designed. The veranda was 13 feet (4 m) wide and all the rooms had high ceilings. A breeze from the river flowed through the open veranda doors and kept the house cool, while the wide veranda kept the house dry even during afternoon showers.

After Mina's death in 1947, Seminole Lodge became a museum and memorial to Edison. All the furnishings and decorations are kept just as they were when Edison and Mina lived there. Every year over 320,000 visitors come to see the house and gardens, as well as the holiday home of Henry Ford, which is next door to Seminole Lodge.

IN THEIR OWN WORDS

"He invents all the while, even in his dreams."

MINA EDISON, DESCRIBING HER HUSBAND.

BELOW: *Edison tests an improved version of his original phonograph, in his laboratory at Seminole Lodge, in 1900.*

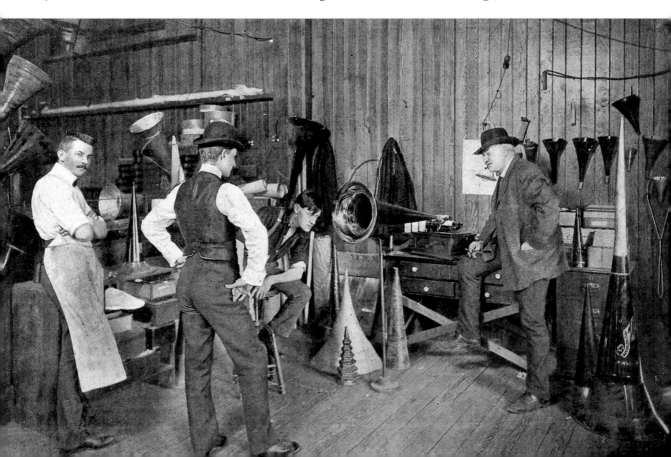

EDISON'S CHILDREN

Edison had six children in all: three (Marion, Tom, and William) from his first marriage to Mary, and three more with Mina (Madeleine, Charles, and Theodore). After his unsuccessful mining venture, Edison was less busy with experiments and business, and he spent more time with his second family than he had with his first. Theodore eventually worked for his father for a while before leaving to set up his own successful research and development company, called Calibron. Charles also became a respected businessman, and at one time was president of Edison's company before becoming governor of New Jersey.

BELOW: *Thomas Edison Jr. (right), Edison's eldest son and second child, whom, he nicknamed "Dash" (his first child, Mary, was nicknamed "Dot"). On the left is William, Edison's third child.*

IN THEIR OWN WORDS

"I see no reason whatever why I should support my son; he has done me no honor and has brought the flush of shame to my cheeks many times…Let [Tom] earn his money like I did. I will continue to send the monthly installment until such time as I think best, but in no case will I loan any more money or increase the monthly amount."

EDISON REPLYING TO HIS DAUGHTER-IN-LAW'S REQUEST THAT HE GIVE TOM MORE MONEY.

Edison did not have good relationships with his older children. He had a falling out with his daughter Marion, who felt hurt when she became ill in Europe and received just "two short letters" from home during her seven-week recovery. Marion returned from Europe in 1892, but soon left and went back to Europe for a second time, eventually marrying a German army officer, Oscar Oeser. Marion lived in Europe until her marriage failed, after World War I.

Tom in particular had a difficult relationship with his father. He once said that Edison had "no more right to be a father than a child of six." The two battled for years over the right to use the Edison name in business. Edison felt his son was ruining his reputation by bringing out badly designed products labeled "Edison," and threatened court action. William also fell out with his father over use of the family name when he tried to bring out an "Edison Spark Plug" for cars. Their quarrel, though, was patched up relatively quickly.

ABOVE: *Edison on his 77th birthday. On Edison's right is his second wife, Mina, with whom he had three more children (Madeleine, Charles, and Theodore).*

THE MAN WHO INVENTED THE FUTURE

In 1913, an article on Edison described him as "this big, smiling, white-haired, blue-eyed, 66-year-old boy." He had lost none of his enthusiasm, but Edison never again came up with a "big trick." The great age of invention was over. New discoveries were made, but they never came one after the other in the way they did during Edison's heyday.

Edison was awarded the Congressional Gold Medal in 1928, in recognition of inventions that "revolutionized civilization." In 1929, he attended a banquet given by President Herbert Hoover to celebrate the fiftieth birthday of the light bulb. In the midst of the celebrations, Edison collapsed. After this, he became increasingly ill.

ABOVE: *This photo, taken on Edison's 82nd birthday, shows him with (left to right) President Herbert Hoover, Henry Ford, and (right) Harvey Firestone. By now Edison was one of the most famous people in the world.*

All his life, Edison had followed the teachings of a man named Cornaro, who thought that people ate far more food than they really needed. For most of his life Edison's daily food was one slice of toast, two glasses of milk, one tablespoon of cooked oats, one tablespoon of chopped spinach, one sardine, and four cookies. He believed that this combination of foods suited his stomach best. In his last years Edison ate just one orange and drank seven glasses of milk each day. By 1931 Edison was suffering from diabetes and a stomach ulcer and, in October, he died.

Soon after Edison's death, President Hoover announced that mourners throughout the United States should turn out their electric lights for one minute. On the evening of October 21, 1931, a wave of darkness swept across the country. The lights went out across the nation as a mark of respect for, as many newspapers claimed at the time, "the man who invented the future."

IN THEIR OWN WORDS

"We are inclined to regard him as one of the wonders of the world."

FROM THE JOURNAL, *Scientific American*, 1878.

LEFT: *Henry Ford talking to Edison, who was almost completely deaf by this time, at the fiftieth anniversary party for Edison's electric light bulb in 1929.*

The Legacy of Edison

THOMAS ALVA EDISON was one of the most remarkable people ever to have lived. There are very few people who can truly be said to have changed the world. Some of them, like Hitler, made the world a worse place for everyone who came into contact with them. Edison made the world a better place for vast numbers of people. He worked on many thousands of ideas throughout his life, and a list of just a few of them is awe-inspiring:

BELOW: *Every night, the New York City skyline and thousands of other cities are a blaze of color—and it was Edison who first lit up New York.*

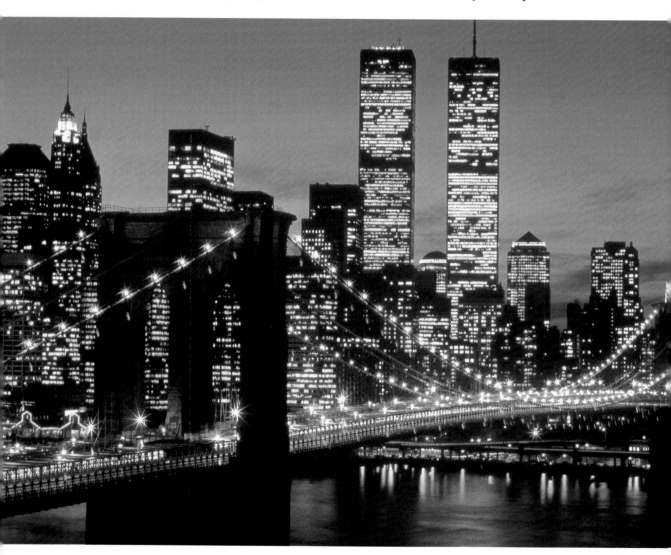

- The adaptations made to the telephone by Edison are still in use today, well over 100 years later. He changed the telephone into a device that allowed people to talk with each other across long distances.

- Edison was one of the first people to bring reliable, safe light and power to homes and businesses in the form of electricity. It's almost impossible now to imagine a world without electricity: There would no flicking a switch to turn on a light, no refrigerated food, no plug-in stereos, computer games, or hair dryers.

- Edison made the first breakthroughs in sound recording, inventing the first device that allowed sound to be recorded and played back. Without this we would have no music from records, CDs, and cassette players, and no sound from televisions or movies.

- The first commercial movies were made in Edison's laboratories. Imagine a world without Hollywood films and all the other movies that are made each year.

Of course, Edison didn't do all the work on all these things alone. He had assistants in his laboratories, and often the ideas had been worked on before by someone else, or were worked on later by other people. But these others might only have worked on one part of, for example, the challenge of electricity. Only Edison was involved in everything; only Edison could really claim to have guided the world into the future.

IN THEIR OWN WORDS

"One day, we may harness the rise and fall of the tides and imprison the rays of the sun."

EDISON IN 1922, AS HE LOOKED FORWARD TO ALTERNATIVE ENERGIES.

BELOW: *A statue of Edison as a young man in Port Huron.*

Timeline

1831

Faraday's Law of Electrical Induction improves the world's understanding of how electricity works.

1847

FEBRUARY 11: Thomas Alva Edison born in Milan, Ohio.

1848

Revolutions sweep across Europe, especially France, Italy, Germany, and the Austro-Hungarian Empire. Gold is discovered in California.

1854

The Edison family moves to Port Huron, Michigan.

1855

Thomas attends school for three months before his mother starts to teach him at home.

1859

Twelve-year-old Edison starts working on the Port Huron–Detroit railway as a newspaper boy.
OCTOBER 17: John Brown seizes government weapons at Harper's Ferry, Virginia, to try and start a slave uprising.
First oil well in Pennsylvania.
Charles Darwin's *The Origin of the Species through Natural Selection* is published.

1860

Abraham Lincoln is elected U.S. President.

1861–65

American Civil War.

1861

JULY 21: Confederate General Robert E. Lee is victorious at the First Battle of Bull Run.

1862

APRIL 6-7: Battle of Shiloh. Edison uses the telegraph to send word of the battle ahead, in order to sell extra newspapers.
AUGUST 27-30: General Lee wins the Second Battle of Bull Run.

1863

Edison becomes a telegrapher, and spends the next few years moving from place to place.
JANUARY 1: President Lincoln proclaims the emancipation of slaves in the U.S.
MAY 1-4: General Lee wins the Battle of Chancellorsville.
JULY 1-3: Confederate army is defeated at the Battle of Gettysburg.

1865

APRIL 9: General Lee surrenders to Union General Ulysses Grant, at Appomatox Courthouse.
APRIL 14: President Lincoln is assassinated in Washington, D.C.

1868

Edison arrives in Boston. He works for the Western Union Telegraph Company and registers his first patent, on his electronic vote recorder.

1869

JANUARY: Edison becomes a freelance inventor. He patents his improvements to the stock ticker.
OCTOBER: Edison and Franklin Pope set up a partnership, which soon dissolves.
Wyoming introduces women's suffrage (the right to vote).

1870–71

War between France and Prussia.

1871

Germany united as one country for the first time.

1871

Edison establishes manufacturing shop in New Jersey.
DECEMBER: Marries Mary Stillwell.

1876

Edison set ups a new laboratory in Menlo Park, New Jersey, which is christened "the invention factory."
MARCH: Alexander Graham Bell patents his telephone.

1877

Edison improves on Bell's telephone.
DECEMBER: Edison invents the phonograph.

1878

Work starts on the electric light system.

1879

OCTOBER: Carbonized string is used as a filament for an electric light bulb.

1880

Electric railway in Menlo Park is demonstrated.

1881

Edison rents a house in Manhattan.

1882

SEPTEMBER 4: Power is switched on at the Pearl Street electric station of the Edison Electric Light Company.

1884

Edison's wife Mary dies.

1885

Karl Benz and Gottlieb Daimler produce the first motor cars in Germany.

1886

Edison marries Mina Miller, and moves to West Orange, New Jersey.

1887

Edison builds a laboratory ten times the size of Menlo Park at West Orange.

1888

Edison begins work on his project to extract iron ore from low-grade deposits in the New Jersey hills.

1891

The kinetoscope is patented.

1893

Recession in the United States.

1898

Spanish-American War. U.S. gains control of Cuba, Puerto Rico, Guam, and the Philippines.

1899

Edison begins work on the electric storage battery for cars and trucks.

1900

Edison, having spent about $2 million, finally abandons his iron-ore project.

1902

Edison sets up a successful cement works. Ideas on road-building and house-building projects came from the cement business, but were not a success.

1910

Edison's first commercial electrical storage battery is released for sale.

1912

Work starts on an electric self-starter for Henry Ford's Model T car.

1913

The Ford Company begins mass production of car parts on an assembly line.

1914–18

World War I rages across Europe and other parts of the world. The U.S. joins the war in 1917. Edison spends much of the war working on U.S. Navy projects.

1917

Revolution in Russia overthrows tsar; Lenin declares a communist regime.

1927

Edison sets up a project in Florida to research home-grown sources of rubber.

1929

OCTOBER: Wall Street Crash sparks Great Depression. U.S. and other economies suffer severe downfalls.

1931

OCTOBER 18: Edison dies. OCTOBER 21: U.S. turns off electric lights as a mark of respect.

Glossary

Battery
An object that stores electricity.

Celluloid film
A substance on which images can be recorded.

Circuit
A system of transporting electricity.

Civil War
A war between different groups of people within one country.

Credit
A loan. If you buy something on credit, you take the goods and pay later.

Diaphragm
A thin skin that vibrates in response to sound.

Dynamo
A device for converting movement into electricity.

Electric current
The movement of electricity from one place to another.

Electrical pulses
Bursts of electrical current.

Electro-mechanician
A person who works on mechanical devices that use electricity.

Electromagnet
A magnet that works only when an electrical current is passing through it.

Industrial
To do with business, trade, or manufacturing.

Filament
A thin strip of material that lights up when electricity passes through it.

Generator
A device that turns heat into movement.

Low-grade
Low-grade metal ore is rock that does not contain much metal.

Manufactured
Made by people instead of occurring naturally.

Mechanical movement
The movement of a machine.

Morse code
A system of representing letters using dots and dashes.

Natural resources
Things such as coal or timber that occur naturally.

Patent
A patent is a legal document, which records the name of the inventor of a new idea.

It entitles the inventor to a share of any money made out of the idea.

Soliciting
To solicit something is to try to get it: For example, a person soliciting your attention is trying to get you to pay them attention.

Stock ticker
A telegraph-based device that transmitted news of the changes in the prices of stocks and shares.

Synchronize
To make things do the same thing at the same time; synchronized watches, for example, tell the same time.

Telegraph
A system of sending messages along a wire using Morse code.

Tramp telegrapher
Someone who moves from place to place working as a telegraph operator.

Transmitted
Sent.

Vacuum
A space in which there is nothing, not even air.

Vote counter
A device for counting votes.

Further Information

BOOKS FOR YOUNGER READERS

Parker, Steve. *Thomas Edison and Electricity.* (Science Discoveries). Pennsylvania: Chelsea House Publications (Library), 1995.

Sproule, Anna. *Thomas A. Edison: Genius With a Bright Idea.* (Giants of Science). Colorado: Blackbirch Marketing, 2000.

BOOKS FOR OLDER READERS

Israel, Paul. Edison: A Life of Invention. New York: John Wiley & Sons, 2000.
Israel uses Edison's personal letters to give insight into what he was thinking. The book is hard work because it's very long, but for anyone especially interested in a particular invention or episode it is useful. There is also a very good index.

WEBSITES

There are lots of Edison websites and most provide links to other sites. Here are a few to start with:

www.edisonian.com/edisonian001.htm
Dedicated to early light bulbs and other inventions.

www.edison.com/kids
A children's site dedicated to Thomas Edison.

www.edison-ford-estate.com
The official website of Edison's former home in Fort Myers, Florida.

Index

Page numbers in **bold** are pages where there is a photograph or an illustration.